M000041431

52 DATES FOR WRITERS

52

DATES FOR
WRITERS

RIDE A TANDEM,
ASSUME AN ALIAS,
AND 50 OTHER WAYS
TO IMPROVE YOUR
NOVEL DRAFT

CLAIRE WINGFIELD

otp

EDINBURGH

Published by
Off the Press Books

Copyright © Claire Wingfield 2013

First published as an ebook in 2013;
first published in paperback edition 2017.

All rights reserved. No part of this publication may be
reproduced, stored in a retrieval system, or transmitted in
any form or by any means, without the prior permission in
writing of Off the Press Books, or as expressly permitted
by law, or under terms agreed with the appropriate
reprographics rights organization.

The author's moral rights have been asserted.

ISBN: 978-0-9575279-1-1

Text design by Couper Street Type Co.
www.couperstreet.com

Typeset in Brandon Grotesque and Sabon

CONTENTS

INTRODUCTION

This book is an invitation to nurture and woo the writer within. It consists of 52 activities for you to get out and do – from climbing a hill to visiting your favourite café, from sampling a new mode of transport to taking part in a hi-tech treasure hunt. Afterwards, you will return to your novel* draft with new insight, fresh material, and stronger writing skills. When you sit down to write, you will have more ideas, greater productivity, and stronger motivation. You may rediscover your passion for a project you thought you were almost done with; or intensify your commitment to finish your work-in-progress, whilst improving your ability to do so.

Each of the 52 dates is designed to give you a creative space away from your everyday life and the daily grind of desk-bound writing. Each is accompanied by a number of exercises, prompts, or observations to help you to focus on one or more areas of your novel. You will be encouraged to look at your writing anew, to be rigorous in testing out your ideas, and – above all – to be playful.

---

* Throughout this book I will most often refer to a novel, though most exercises will work equally well for a short story or series of short stories or even narrative non-fiction such as a biography or memoir.

Perhaps you are lost somewhere in the middle of a draft, or feeling daunted at the beginning or end of such a feat as writing a novel, and a process once sparked by passion feels a long way from being playful. But all writers must play, if their imagination is to be agile enough to fulfill the task they have set themselves.

Each writing date you go on has the potential to bring something new, unexpected and unique to your writing. You might also find the time, space and enthusiasm to explore something you already carry with you, but is not yet present in your draft.

You could, of course, plan to work through one date each week for a year. Or one every two weeks, or simply begin by picking several that tackle a particular area of your manuscript, or your writing in general, that you'd like to explore. For this purpose, each date is assigned a key indicating the writing skill or area of novel writing it focuses on, and there is a table at the beginning of the book, showing which writing dates address which areas. For those days you are unable to get out of the house, or simply have less time, the table also highlights a number of dates better suited to taking place at home.

Many of the dates and accompanying activities will help you in developing a particular facet of your novel – such as character, plot, or setting. They will bring richness and specificity to these areas, and allow you to think through them away from the restraints of what you already have on the page.

Many will also encourage you to bring an analytical eye to what you have already written, helping you to view your work as though you were a reader fresh to your writing.

There are also a number of dates which deal with the business of being a writer – finding time to write and staying motivated, making submissions and marketing your work.

Each will be useful to you at a different stage – and some exercises you may wish to return to as your draft progresses.

Not all of the work you complete will find its way into your novel. Some will refuel your imagination, encourage you to reflect on your craft, or spark new ideas entirely. Sometimes you might write copious new material, and eventually edit it down to a single paragraph for your final draft. After the 52 dates, there is a short essay on editing to help you think about integrating fresh work into your novel draft, and to support you in achieving a satisfyingly coherent and focused final product.

At the very end of the book, there are a number of examples, so you can see how a particular activity might work on a particular text. I have picked three well-known novels of different genres, all of which have been in the UK best-seller list in the last 15 years; as well as one novel that was once a commercial flop but has become an enduring classic. These are separate from the main body of the text, so as not to inhibit your ideas and creativity, and in case anyone is keen not to read the spoilers* these include. The novels are:

Atonement by Ian McEwan
Harry Potter and the Philosopher's Stone
by J.K. Rowling
The Girl with the Dragon Tattoo by Steig Larsson
The Great Gatsby by F. Scott Fitzgerald

---

* The main body of this book also includes spoilers for season one of TV thrillers *Broen* (*The Bridge*) and *Forbrydelsen* (*The Killing*). You have been warned!

As with any handbook, it is easy to simply read through the ideas, walking through the actions in your mind perhaps, rather than in real life. And perhaps for many writers of fiction, used to keeping their work in their heads and at their desks, this is an even more tempting approach. You may find, for instance, that in browsing through this book an exercise appeals and you could sit down and complete it right away. Instead, start a Writing Log, and record any ideas sparked by the process – right from the first reading of the book. It might also help to have ready a large roll of paper for the activities linked to the dates, as you will need plenty of space for your ideas.

All that is left to do after that is to take out your diary and mark down when you will go on that date!

KEY CHART

CHARACTERIZATION

1* 10 15 22 25 30 52

PLOT

1* 3 10 12 16* 18 20 23 32 33
34 36 38 39 41 43 44 47 50 52

SETTING

2 4 5 6 8 9 11* 16* 17 18 21
23 26* 28 31 32 36 47 51 52

STYLE

1* 4 7 13 14 19 29 30 32 33
37 38 40 42 45 46 48 51 52

WRITING BUSINESS

6* 7 9 12 24 27 35 49 52

* These writing dates can be carried out at home.

COOK
SOMETHING
LUXURIOUS

Whether it's a new recipe or an old favourite; whether you eat alone or with company; whether the attempt goes awry or perfectly to plan, savour the preparation and the results, and at some point afterwards:

Write about the role of food in your novel.

Your characters' relationships with food can evoke setting, bring an awareness of dominant and counter cultures to the fore, and betray their passions and anxieties. For example, does your office worker resist the daily cake round or readily indulge? What does your teenage protagonist spend their lunch money on? Which of your characters is a cautious, faddy or adventurous eater, and why? If you don't know the answers to these questions, try writing a food biography for each of your central characters. Consider such questions as:

What is this character's earliest food memory?

Who taught them to cook?

Who do they cook for?

Who cooks for them?

What role does food play in their culture?

Does this character cook from taste or recipe?

Convenience foods or home-cooking?

How extravagant is their weekday lunch?

Any weekend or holiday food rituals?

Now you have an enhanced knowledge of your characters' eating habits, take a closer look at a mealtime / refreshment scene you've already drafted. As the daily activity of eating is so familiar to us, these can sometimes suffer from underwriting, with a sketch given of a generic bar / meal scene. Can you bring more precision to your writing here?

To generate some new material, you might:

Set two of your characters into conflict on a food-related matter.

GO
GEOCACHING

Register at www.geocaching.com to enjoy the thrill of tracking down a hidden cache following coordinates sent to a GPS device or smartphone. Whether you begin your adventure on your doorstep or further afield, your hi-tech treasure hunt can help to put you in the position of your reader – who must navigate your novel using the clues you provide.

Afterwards:

> Conduct a survey of the major revelations of your novel. Make a list / chart of where the key information in your novel is revealed. Is it all bunched up near the beginning, or in certain chapters? Make note of the clues you leave before any revelations, as well as the questions the novel raises concerning your plot. Pay special attention to the end pay-off.

Having the facts about the challenge you are setting your readers laid out in front of you will make it easier to plan any adjustments. It's important to have a handle on this, because the excitement of 'solving' your novel is what keeps your reader with you. Whilst most obvious for a crime novel or thriller, all writers must ration the information they provide to their readers, and think carefully about the order and pace of each new revelation.

You might also:

> Record your adventure on the geocaching website and in your Writing Log.

 See Example Texts

 View geocaching pictures and stories at www.geocaching.com

ATTEND A CELEBRITY APPEARANCE

No matter if you celebrate or scorn modern celebrity culture, there's something worth learning from the cult itself. Looming large in modern life, attracting the fickle beacon of public attention, a little time observing one of these feted individuals can make you ask the question every writer must. *Do I have a character worth writing about?*

At its most basic, the question invites some reflection on what sets your character apart. For the celebrity you have encountered, the answer might be: their ambition, their talent, their failings, their failures – all magnified or manufactured for public consumption. And what of your character? What is the quirk or nub that sets him or her apart – and *will this get through to your reader?* To help make sure of this:

> Plan one change to give greater definition to one of your central characters – a detail that really makes this character stand out.

 See Example Texts

Perhaps you observed others in attendance at your celebrity event, their interest ranging from the curious to the fanatical. What was it that claimed their attention? The charisma, talent or allure of the individual; or the pull of the narrative of triumph and tragedy that surrounds them? You might ask this same question of your own protagonist – for ultimately, your readers' interest must also span from curiosity to fanaticism.

Of course, most of us have mixed feelings towards our celebrities. Do we admire, despise, pity or envy them? The characters that most enthrall inspire something of all of these emotions. But what if we adjust the balance?

> Thinking of your novel, how much of the time do you expect your reader to admire your central character? Come up with a percentage. And how much of the time do you expect your reader to despise your main character? Again, come up with a percentage.

> Reverse these percentages. What changes to the novel would be required to achieve this?

> Re-write one of your key scenes to satisfy this new balance.

> You might repeat this exercise using 'envy' and 'pity'.

CLIMB A HILL OR RIDE A FERRIS WHEEL

View things from a new perspective, and afterwards:

Choose a section from your novel to write or re-write from this expanded viewpoint. What can you zoom out to include? For example, a scene of two people dining in a restaurant might move first to the other diners, then to the restaurant kitchen, then the adjoining street, and out to the neighbourhood and surrounding area, ad infinitum. What's happening in each of these places? What do they tell you about the world of your novel? That street, for example, might be almost empty, or full of luxury cars your protagonist can only dream of owning, or of old bangers and your protagonist has rolled up in a show-stopping sports car. There might be a burglary taking place, or a proposal – or a murder.

Experiment with zooming in on different moments in the novel, too. What do you see? That same restaurant scene might reveal the stain on her blouse your protagonist is trying to hide, the poster in the men's room, the carefully chosen wine glasses or carelessly stacked chairs. Or, by zooming in, you might find yourself inspired to allow the colour of the walls to seep into the scene – creating a powerful emotional charge.

It's easy to stay in one fairly safe descriptive mode throughout your novel. Experimenting with perspective can help you develop an interesting and distinctive style. You might not directly use all of this material, but by both opening out and focusing in on key parts of your novel, you will certainly spark some fresh ideas.

VISIT A CREMATORIUM OR GRAVEYARD

The barest detail on a gravestone can move or intrigue us, or send a shiver down a spine. Make note of those markings or entries that stayed with you, and then, in a free-writing exercise, take an hour to:

> Write something inspired by your visit.

Turn your thoughts to your novel, and to the losses endured by your characters. What different beliefs and attitudes towards death do they hold? How openly, and in what ways do they grieve?

Death brings family relationships into stark relief, and places them under pressure. To explore this:

> Write a scene in which your protagonist travels in the funeral car of a family member.

The deathbed can also bring unlikely soothsayers. Disappointments and long-held grievances may finally be aired, or ominous warnings issued. To give this a supernatural twist:

> Create a ghost to haunt one of your characters. The
> ghost brings a warning of a choice your character
> must make – one thing they must do differently to
> change the outcome of the novel. Write an encounter
> between the ghost and your character.

Whilst you might not transfer the idea of a ghost to your draft, this juncture where the novel could have come to a different conclusion had your protagonist made a different choice is an important one.

 The Trick is to Keep Breathing by Janice Galloway is a harrowing and breathtakingly inventive portrayal of grief.

TRANSFORM YOUR WRITING SPACE

Making space for writing is sometimes one of the most difficult things a writer can do. For all of us there are days when we would rather not sit at our desk – especially if we work another job that is also deskbound. Whilst many of the dates in this book are an antidote to the sitting writer, there are inevitably hours when we must pound the keys, or perhaps for a few of us, scribble away.

This date invites you to pay attention to where you write when you must cover some distance, to think about how you can create an environment conducive to this.

> Decide on a colour to symbolize your novel and incorporate it into your writing space. This might change as you work through different sections of your novel. Take a photo before each change, to document your changing space.
>
> Create a writing date table, on which you can display objects from your dates.

Keep a Writing Log* visible and update it often.

Make one other change to your writing space.

You might also:

Reverse your preferences to work in order or chaos for as long as you can bear. If you prefer to tidy your desk at the end of every writing session, leave it messy. You may find an unexpected jostling of objects or notes gives you a new idea. If you prefer to keep your writing tools and notes spread out where you can see them, focus on bringing order to your workspace. You may find the discipline of tidying your work away each day helps bring a new clarity to your work and goals.

Changing your writing space is also a good way to mark the beginning of work on a new manuscript, or a distinction between different projects.

---

* I'm sometimes asked what to include in a Writing Log. The idea is simply to ensure you have a space to record *whatever seems useful to you* of the process of engaging in the writing dates, or revising your novel. What we record is often what we accomplish, and simply keeping a Writing Log can add accountability for your writing goals. A record of the process can help you identify the anxieties and obstacles you face as a writer, as well as what motivates and inspires you, and how and when you are at your most productive or creative (which unfortunately may not coincide). You might want to keep a track of your progress in terms of word count or tasks ticked off, or you might decide to capture your feelings about your draft, or to note down the fresh decisions you have made. You may find yourself writing fragments of your novel, or those details you encounter in your day-to-day life that seem to you to belong to the world of your narrative. Whether you write just a few words to 'sign in' each day, or find reward in writing a longer account of your work, the Writing Log is an incredibly personal document. It is also something you can always turn back to.

SWIM IN
COLD WATER

Document your swim.

You'll be following many artists and writers before you – perhaps Byron with his Hellespont crossing being the most famous – in channeling the rejuvenating effects of a dip in open water to spark or revive your creativity. You might use this as the diving off point for an article for local press, a writing magazine, or your own writing blog or website. It's never too early to start to build a readership and a buzz around your work. Just make sure you keep a full database of contacts / potential readers from any publicity you undertake.

A swim in the wild is also often chosen as a moment of renewal at the turn of the year, and both festive dippers and devotees note the welcome reawakening of senses dulled by day-to-day life. So, after the goosebumps have subsided:

Write a scene from your novel, paying heightened attention to the senses.

Wait a day or two, then rewrite it, further exaggerating the senses. (You might need to turn off that pesky inner editor to really embrace this exercise.)

Make a list of phrases or ideas from this exercise you might transfer to your novel.

 www.outdoorswimmingsociety.com has tips on safety and making the most of your swim.

ATTEND A
TWO-TEAM
SPORTS FIXTURE

Soak up the atmosphere, the rivalry, the drama of the sporting match, and afterwards:

> If your novel features an antagonist*, think about how evenly they and your protagonist are matched. Are the two truly worthy opponents? Not sure? Make a record of antagonist–protagonist 'matches', split into a single season – or many.

---

* If your novel does not contain a specific antagonist, try grouping together the factors that stand in the way of your protagonist's goals. You might discover a clear antagonist – symbolic or otherwise – would be a strong addition to your novel.

Thinking of your novel as a series of 'fixtures' between the two sides allows you to include the cheerleaders, fans and supporting players to both sides. Each 'match report' can also include their contribution to the game.

Analyze the results. You might discover the protagonist–antagonist encounters you have set up through the novel are not true 'matches'. Plan at least three changes to intensify the rivalry between the two teams. Make sure you offer the fans of both sides an exhilarating showdown.

 See Example Texts

GO BOOK
BROWSING

Go with no buying agenda, and with plenty of time to spare. Linger in departments you don't usually visit; revisit past passions; take note of titles that compel you to take a closer look, blurbs that have you thumbing through to the opening pages, opening pages that immerse you in the world of this author, this book. You might notice a beautiful cover design, or a tempting store promotion. You might stake out the section *your* book belongs in, surreptitiously observing the habits of other book buyers.

At home, browse the online stores. Include e-books in your search. Again, try to look outside your usual buying habits, and see what sparks your interest.

Afterwards:

> Spend some time thinking about what you hope to achieve with your work. How do you want your readers to feel – about your characters; about the events of the novel? At the end of the book, what do you want

a reader to take away with them? What's important to you in terms of the mood / tone of the piece? Write a summary of your thoughts on this. Keep it somewhere you can see it often.

Thinking of your current draft, decide on three things you can change to better meet your aims.

You might try writing a blurb for your novel.

Whilst this isn't the same as the synopsis* publishers and literary agents usually require with submissions, a compelling introduction to your work can be used in submissions cover letters or in marketing a self-published novel, as well as simply giving you confidence in discussing your work with any potential reader.

Afterwards, you might:

Work your blurb into a pitch of 25 words.

Write a second and third 25-word pitch, taking a different angle for your introduction in each of these.

It's important for you to be able to confidently introduce your work. The 25-word pitch encourages you to be concise

---

* A synopsis is an outline of the plot, in the order in which it occurs, including the ending. Usually 1–3 double-spaced pages in length, though check publisher / agent requirements. A synopsis is focused on plot only – no need to include anything on style, or how your reader should interpret your work, or the process of writing the novel. The best synopses convey a sense of the writer's unique voice, and the style of the novel, in the way in which they are written.

(nothing worse than talking about your work, and realizing you have lost your listener), and having more than one version encourages you to be versatile – to match the pitch to the person you are pitching to. It also encourages you to interrogate your novel's selling points. If you are having trouble with this, or are at a very early stage in your novel's development, a good starting point is to write a pitch in the same format for several novels you know well.

VISIT A FOREST OR OTHER WILD PLACE

Afterwards, write a scene in which you are invited (willingly or under duress) to share a meal with one of its inhabitants.

This scene will be one in which the protagonist (you!) is granted access to somewhere that is usually closed / hidden. Somewhere forbidden, or at least, unseen.

Returning to your work-in-progress, it's worth thinking about where and what your central character has access to. Does your central character provide a novice perspective on the novel's environment (like you, learning the ways of the forest dweller) or are they already part of the scenery (the falcon who may share its kill with you)? If you are introducing an unfamiliar world to your readers or wish to throw a new perspective on the familiar, it can work well for your protagonist to provide an outsider's view. This allows your reader to be initiated in the ways of that world (or accept a new perspective) at the same time as your protagonist, and can prevent your descriptive material feeling forced. An example of this is Harry Potter comparing quidditch to basketball for the reader, which works as he is entirely new to the wizarding world. Another strong example is *Into the Wild*, the first of the Warrior Cats series, in which household 'kittypet' Rusty joins a clan of wild cats and is reborn as the warrior FirePaw – allowing the reader to be initiated into the rituals of clan life at the same time as he is.

CURL UP WITH A FAVOURITE NOVEL

But keep a pen and paper to hand to make note of the major plot developments as you read. You'll need to find your flow here – perhaps read two chapters, then go back and make notes. Break these notes into a bullet-point synopsis of the 'spine' of the book. If you can, try to keep this to just a few words to show the major plot developments. Here's an example, looking at chapter one of *Harry Potter and the Philosopher's Stone*:

1
Meet the Dursleys and son Dudley
…who are ashamed of their relatives, the Potters.
Follow Mr Dursley as he sees:
    Tawny owl
    Cat reading a map
    People in cloaks talking about a Harry Potter!
    First mention of 'muggles'.

Voldemort introduced (so frightening many will not say his name).
Voldemort killed Lily and James Potter!
But baby Harry survived!

Harry will be famous in the wizarding world!
But it is decided he must live in obscurity with his aunt and uncle, the Dursleys!

You can see some of the important elements of good fiction here: the unusual, the unexpected, looming threats, life-changing choices – and the full synopsis shows clearly how and where the threats multiply and the drama escalates.

Here's a similar approach used with *The Great Gatsby* – although to demonstrate a different way of presenting this, each point is longer and quotations are included:

I

Narrator introduces Gatsby, a man of a 'romantic readiness such as I have never found in any person and which it is not likely I shall ever find again.'

Dinner with the excessively wealthy Buchanans – Tom, 'one of the most powerful ends that ever played football at New Haven' and his enchanting wife Daisy (Miss Baker also present).

Dinner interrupted by the telephone – 'Tom's got some woman in New York.'

Discovery that Jordan Baker is a golfing star, and Daisy intends to set her and Nick up.

Back home, Nick sees Gatsby on his lawn, stretching his arms towards a green light across the dock, trembling.

2

Nick meets Tom's mistress, Myrtle. Tom propositions her right in front of her husband's eyes.

The three travel to New York together; Tom buys Myrtle a dog.

A drunken night ends in an argument about Daisy. Tom breaks Myrtle's nose!

3

Nick is invited to one of Gatsby's extravagant parties, and runs into Jordan Baker.

The party is transformed into 'something significant, elemental and profound' (p.48), just as Nick meets his host for the first time.

Gatsby calls Jordan away, and she returns to hint at a secret.

Nick realises the truth behind a scandal.

Note the extravagance of characterisation – the excessively wealthy Gatsby is unlike anyone the narrator has ever met before, and Tom has a rare sporting accolade to his name. Note too the urgency to the plot developments – dinner interrupted by a mistress; the mistress propositioned beneath her husband's nose; a man breaking his lover's nose – there is no holding back here! And then the secrets and scandals – more of the ingredients of good fiction.

Breaking down a number of novels in this way can really help you focus on what works in writing fiction.

As an extension to this exercise, you might choose to concentrate on different aspects of a novel – such as including notes on style, or simply recording your responses to the novel as you read. It can be extremely illuminating to have a record of your experiences as a reader – for example, making sense of characters or your predictions on how the plot will unfold. These are moments when you have fully entered into the world of the novel. And this is what all readers – and writers – are searching for.

A further use of this technique is to analyse the pace of different novels, and begin to think about this in relation to your own work. Perhaps one thing to realize is just how many plot developments can be packed into a novel – leaving you to check you genuinely have enough material in your own plotline. A good way to do this is to complete a similar bullet-point synopsis for your own work, and compare it to several you have prepared for works of the same genre. You can also use the bullet-point synopsis when brainstorming and testing out revisions – or when planning your novel.

Seeing the bare bones of your novel like this can also alert you to areas you might need to work on – points where the draft doesn't meet your ambitions for it, for example, or anywhere the tension or drama dips. Don't be disheartened if this is the case, but do make plans to tackle these issues.

For now:

Make note of any ideas or amendments suggested by your reading.

 See Date 17: Take a Different Route Home

DAYDREAM

Return to heady teenage days, and devote yourself to some unfettered daydreaming. If this is a forgotten luxury, remember how you used to daydream. A monotonous task can simulate the boredom of the classroom. A special place can recapture the romanticism of youth. Simply being still can help to recover that sense of endless time, with plenty enough to dream.

Afterwards, take a leaf from those striving for sports or business success and visualize your successfully completed novel. Write the dedication, imagine the cover design, walk through your first book signing. To build your resilience as a writer and an artist:

> Write your own mantra. Get into the habit of using it often, and it will keep you going when you may be in danger of allowing work on your manuscript to drift.

> The next step is to create a set of mantras, print or write them onto card, and pick one to support you through each day of your writing journey. Prompts to help you write your mantras: What have you learnt on

your writing journey? Where did you feel like giving up? What kept you going then, and what keeps you writing now?

You might extend this to think about the dreams of your characters. Do they have time to daydream? How determined are they? Who supports their dreams and who sees them as a folly? What would they have to do to achieve their dreams?

A sentence at a time
I will tell my story
Create first (edit later)

VISIT AN ART GALLERY OR EXHIBITION

Take some time out to lose yourself in an exhibition or gallery – simply enjoying another art form is wonderful food for a writer. Focusing on what you can *see* also increases your awareness of the visual element of your novel. At home, you might:

Consider a key scene from your novel. What do you invite your reader to see, and what do you leave them to fill in for themselves?

Write a hyper-visual version of the scene (the novels of artist Salvador Dali provide an interesting model for this), followed by a draft with all visual detail stripped away.

There's a fine balance to be found, but many writers give minimal – or patchy – visual direction, missing an important opportunity to engage the mind's eye. It's worth experimenting to find your own style here – crucially, one that fits your novel, as well as what you hope to achieve in your writing.

As someone who works with the written word, how much attention did you pay to the titles or descriptions accompanying the artwork? Once at home, could you remember any fragments of text? Perhaps you felt compelled to note some down during your visit – reminding us how just a few words can have a powerful emotional significance. Whilst there can be a pleasing poetry to the title of a work of art, or an intriguing story told in the accompanying description, most often the artist will steer clear of too many words in favour of leaving room for the viewer's interpretation. If we think of the role of the literary scholar or critic, we are reminded that just as a great work of art ignites debate, great fiction inspires discussion. In neither case is this possible if we are told exactly what to think. Just as viewing a painting or a sculpture requires active participation from the viewer, so too must a reader engage in an active reading experience. And writers must leave room for this.

> Look again at a key scene from your novel. Are you
> telling the reader how to interpret it? Where can you
> create ambiguity? Beware exclamation marks telling a
> reader that a plot development is exciting or surprising,
> for example; or telling your reader how to interpret the
> actions of your characters. In each case, a reader must
> be allowed to make up their own mind.

If you find this a difficult task, you might think of a child's early classroom encounters with literature. One of the many ways books are used in the classroom is to start a discussion. On a line-by-line basis, a teacher might ask: why do you think the character did that? A good writer will have left some wonderfully evocative clues but steered clear of giving a definitive answer.

 See Date 14: Go Star Gazing or Visit a Stone Circle

 Ways of Seeing by John Berger

GO STAR GAZING OR VISIT A STONE CIRCLE

Soak up the celestial, or the silent mysteries of the stone circle to retune your sense of the universe. While you are there:

> Reflect upon the key themes and ideas of your novel.

> Next, focus your thoughts to one or two symbols or images you might use to communicate these key themes or ideas.

For example, in F. Scott Fitzgerald's enduring favourite *The Great Gatsby*, Jay Gatsby's impossible romantic longing is represented by 'a single green light, minute and far away'. This image is prominently placed at the end of the first chapter, and there are repeated references to the green light throughout the novel.

Once you have a well-developed sense of the themes and ideas of your novel, as well as the symbolism you want to achieve, it will be easier to pick out what to focus on in your descriptions. This will help you to ensure that all material is working to give the novel resonance, and to avoid sections that are merely 'padding' – without true significance.

You might also:

> Ask of your novel: what are the unknowns, the unknowable? This could be something beyond the end of the narrative (will the newly-weds live on happily together?); a question left deliberately unanswered at the novel's conclusion (which choice will the protagonist make?); or something from earlier in the novel, such as a missing motive (what really drove that character to kill?). Readers want answers, and sometimes not providing them can make a novel live on past the final page. (Think of a news story eked out by the media – the most absorbing narratives, the ones we might return to in our thoughts years later, can be the ones with no clear answer.)

> Ask the same of another novel in your genre.

There's magic in the unknown; a brooding fertility in the unknowable which can work on the reader's imagination long after a book is finished. If this isn't something you are tapping into:

> Make notes on where you might explore this.

 See Date 13: Visit an Art Gallery or Exhibition

To gain new insights into the world of your novel, and the laws or rules it is governed by, you might:

> Rewrite one of your key scenes as a scene from a science-fiction novel. If your novel already is this genre, rewrite a key scene in the style of a romantic comedy.

TAKE A TOUR
OF YOUR
HOME TOWN

Before you set off:

Note down what you are about to see. Try to include as much detail as you can remember. An urban tour might include street names, shops you might pass, postboxes, grassy areas, the trees that mark the route.

Using your notes, write a short description of the route from the Point of View of either: a child riding a horse; a passenger in an articulated lorry; an animal of your choice.

Afterwards:

Note down where you can expand or improve on your original description.

Sketch out a character based on this location. The character could become the starting point for a short story or, if your home area features in your novel, you might work on giving this location a greater voice in the novel, or create a minor character that embodies the characteristics of place.

You might also:

Give the location of your novel a voice and invite them to confide their thoughts on the events of the novel. Is the city determinedly indifferent, friend or foe?

 Three classic novels in which location becomes character are Virginia Woolf's *Orlando*, Thomas Hardy's *The Mayor of Casterbridge* and Monica Ali's *Brick Lane*.

BROWSE OLD PHOTOGRAPHS

Afterwards:

Write a short story about someone in the photographs you do not recognize.

Create a family tree for one of your characters. For each entry, include note of the family traits and physical resemblances that have been inherited, as well as any stories that have become family folklore, passed through the generations.

Write a scene that features a photo album belonging to your protagonist.

You might also:

Write a scene in which one or more of your protagonist's ancestors appear.

Write a scene in which there is conflict over an inheritance of something other than money.

TAKE A
DIFFERENT
ROUTE HOME

The slightest detour to our daily routine can bring a fresh perspective, and open our minds to new possibilities. Afterwards:

> Working away from your novel draft, rewrite your favourite scene so the events of the novel take an entirely different course.

Next:

> Assemble a fresh plot outline, taking in the consequences of the radically revised scene. Be playful with it – change as much of the plotline as you feel comfortable with, or inclined to. Complete the plot outline to the end of the novel, beginning each

line after the first AND (intensifications; additional information); BUT (surprises; obstacles); OR (a choice of developments). You can mark surprises or twists with an exclamation mark, and use bold type to indicate key threads / developments. In creating a fresh plotline, take inspiration from the key words: intensification; revelation; resolution; mystery; surprise; challenge; obstacle; antagonist...

 See Date 11: Curl up with a Favourite Novel

Any writer will know that it is entirely possible to become too attached to your words – especially when they can look so neat and final on a screen in front of you. (Another reason escaping the desk is a good habit to cultivate; and why it can work well to write by hand sometimes, despite all the technology available to us.)

Creating an alternative plotline like this can help you to escape a rut or to solve a problem in the narrative, as well as give you greater confidence in your choices. Even if your plot-line ultimately remains unchanged, the awareness of different outcomes will give an additional layer and potency to your novel.

VISIT A
FORTUNE-TELLER

First:

> Write down your feelings and an account of how you imagine the visit will unfold. Describe the fortune-teller you imagine you will meet, the room as you imagine it will be...

All forms of fortune-telling hold Life's big events in stark relief – and for many it is an experience preceded by fears, anticipation and superstition; perhaps met with a giddiness, skepticism and refusal to take heed of any warnings. After your visit:

> Write a scene in which one of your characters is confronted with the consequences of their actions by a fortune-teller or in a crystal ball.

This is a reminder of how well stories can work when a character refuses to take notice of a forewarning; of how much a reader can become emotionally involved when a character is blundering on regardless, and the signs are all there for a disaster of considerable magnitude. Where you can hardly concentrate for wanting to direct your character's attention to what is only too obvious. And still the action moves forward and the catastrophe approaches. This is the basis of Greek tragedy, and it is worth returning to.

Fortune-telling is also an apt analogy for novel writing, in the sense that the end of a novel is often in its beginning. The future has been told in those opening pages, and it is a test of the reader's skill whether they will see this. (Again, these are the kinds of books a reader will wish to return to.)

As in Greek tragedy, where readers know or suspect the outcome from the very beginning, the tension and the interest is in exactly *how* events unfold in order to reach the future that has been foretold.

If the end of a novel is often in its beginning, it is also often – and equally powerfully – buried in character. In this sense, the layers of character must be peeled away to reveal a hidden core which has more influence over events than may at first be apparent. This is a character's fatal flaw.

For example, in the first series of the Danish TV thriller *The Killing*, a young girl is killed and we follow her parents in their grief, as well as the investigation as it twists and turns. We see the parents grow apart, the father silent and brooding in his grief, the mother unable to turn her eyes from the investigation as it takes in her daughter's school friends, the politician she had been having an affair with, the strip club she had secretly worked at. Finally, the finger is pointed at one of the family's own employees – a man who is almost part of the family – and at the story's conclusion we discover it is the father's past of violent racism, which the viewer has already glimpsed, which provided the motivation for the murder. Though the reader has been placed to have a great deal of pity for him, the father's fatal flaw of racism and barely suppressed violence provides the key to the narrative. This combination of someone who commands sympathy and yet is shown to be the cause of their own suffering is a powerful one, and makes the father of the murdered girl a compelling tragic hero.

The tradition is followed in *The Bridge*, a second Nordic thriller, in which an investigation of a body made up of two halves – one from Denmark and one from Sweden – is found on the bridge linking the two countries, thus necessitating the cooperation of the two countries' investigative forces. This time, despite the investigation taking the expected twists and turns, the fatal flaw is the infidelity of one of the detectives – again, glimpsed by the viewer long before its part in the murders becomes clear; and again, powerfully combined with a hefty dose of pity for the character.

So, two fatal flaws at the heart of two murder investigations.

Your novel may not be of the genre to create a tragic hero, but it is worth pausing at this point to:

Write about your protagonist's weakness or tragic flaw.

 One of the Greek tragedies, such as *Oedipus Rex* by Sophocles.

ATTEND A CONCERT

Afterwards, think about the soundscape of your novel. Sounds of nature, man-made sounds, the music of celebration or of mourning. What do your protagonists hear, and what will you share with your reader? To help you with this:

Pick three important locations from your novel and list the sounds that belong to each of them.

Pick one of your key scenes or chapters and plot its soundscape.

Revise the scene or chapter using this fresh knowledge.

You can extend this approach out to the full novel. You might also:

Write your novel as the lyrics of a song or the score of a symphony.

ASSUME AN ALIAS

You might arrange a situation where others are also 'in character' – such as a murder mystery party – or you might simply set yourself a task to undertake as a fictitious character. The next step is to:

> Choose a particular time and day, and go about the day as you could reasonably expect one of your central characters to. Try to make all decisions, reactions and interactions as your character would. If it is the weekend, what would your character choose or be obliged to do? If they would read the newspaper, for example, read the publication they would choose in the way they would read it. (Online? On what kind of device? Print? Which sections?) If it is a lunch break at work, how would your character spend this?

Getting under your character's skin is of course crucial in creating a credible world for your novel. And even though some writers might find this task an uncomfortable one, it reminds us of an important truth: *your character is not you.*

If, for example, you felt your character's Sunday morning routine would be very similar to your own, and that indeed your reading choices and the implied allegiances therein would be one and the same, this may indicate you need to bring your character further from your own life choices and opinions.

For everyone, the discipline of 'living out' the character you have created can help you make credible choices for your character in your draft, as well as increase your sensitivity towards the Point of View you are writing from.

 See Date 51: Listen to a Professional Storyteller

TAKE A MODE OF TRANSPORT YOU'VE NEVER TRAVELLED BY BEFORE

A segway, a rickshaw, a golf buggy, a light aircraft, a camel
… enjoy the journey and afterwards:

> Write a scene in which one of your characters creates
> a stir with their unusual method of transportation.

Next, to test your writing mettle:

> Plan and write an extended scene or a short story in
> which a journey by a common mode of transport is
> infused with drama.

An excellent example of a journey seething with emotional significance appears in the opening pages of Esther Freud's coming-of-age tale, *Love Falls*. In the novel, seventeen-year-old Lara travels by train from London to Italy with the father she hardly knows.

BROWSE A FLEA MARKET OR CAR BOOT SALE

Afterwards:

> Write about one of the objects you saw. Give it an instrumental role in your novel.
>
> Make notes on the objects that are important to your novel. You might draw or paint these.

Novelist Orhan Pamuk enlisted visual artists to construct items from his novel *The Museum of Innocence*, including symbolic objects, such as a 'Black Light Machine' representing his protagonist's nighttime melancholy and a white porcelain 'broken' heart. These objects and many others sourced by the novelist are displayed in a museum in Istanbul housing objects belonging to the novel's narrator, Kemal, who amasses an enormous collection related to his dead beloved and to the era in which he loved her. Every purchase of the novel includes a ticket to the real-life museum.

 See Example Texts

ATTEND AN EVENT OF GRAND PROPORTIONS

Seek out a moment of celebration, spectacle and ambition such as a carnival, or the opening to a festival or sporting event. An echo of the jaw-dropping ambition of the opening ceremony to an Olympic Games, for example, can also be found in any sporting event which is preceded by a moment of ceremony – such as the singing of the National Anthem before a football match.

Afterwards, consider the idea of spectacle or great achievement in relation to your work. If there is already such a moment in your novel, think about how you can make that moment even bigger, and better defined. Have you fully explored the meaning behind that display of powerful ambition and achievement?

Next:

Write a scene in which one of your characters (and
if you can't choose, pick your protagonist) is offered
one of the biggest (and most public) jobs in the world.
Curating a royal wedding, directing that opening
Olympic ceremony – something to match those grand
proportions. Would your character do his or her best to
duck out of it; or would they embrace the challenge in
a spirit of humility or conceit?

You might make this the basis of a short story, or simply
allow the new insights into your character to filter into your
work.

It is likely that an event on a grand scale trumpets a beginning of significance – as we see in weddings, births, and
Olympic ceremonies – so it's worth pausing to think of the
opening of your novel, and how it sets your reader up for
what is to come. Is there evidence of a quiet or grand ambition
behind your beginning?

TAKE A
WRITING RETREAT

With all the ideas generated from your writing dates, you'll need some time get those words down. You might sign up for an organized retreat, or you might make your own – tailoring the break to meet the needs of you and your writing. You might take yourself to new surroundings, or simply clear some space at home. The important thing is that you tell those who need to know that you are dedicating a set number of hours per day to your writing and are not to be disturbed! You could take a full week of holiday for your writing retreat (writing in the morning or afternoon, for example – and doing something which will replenish your creativity in the second part of the day), or take two weekends if this isn't possible. If you struggle to set aside a large amount of time in one go like this, you might stretch your writing retreat over e.g. 2 weeks, spending for example 2–3 hours per evening or morning on your writing for a set number of days each week. Be flexible and realistic about what will best suit your lifestyle. Preparation is key in making sure you feel able to immerse yourself in your writing during your 'retreat' – so, as much as possible, get any chores or responsibilities that would intrude on your creative space out of the way.

You could even organize a retreat with some writing friends if this would motivate rather than distract you – checking in daily online, for example, or finding somewhere to get together.

Use your writing retreat to continue to nourish yourself as a writer. If you are able to dedicate full days to a retreat, you might focus on your word count in the morning / evening, leaving you a few hours in the afternoon to fill. Don't over-stretch yourself in your 'free' time – ideal activities are those that will allow your ideas to gently percolate. Some ideas are:

Going for a walk or cycle ride

Cooking

Writing a letter

One or two structured writing exercises (particularly if you are working as a group)

Reading (including books on the craft of writing)

Any other form of rest

Afterwards, get out your diary and block in further retreats. If you don't have a regular writing habit already, you might use the retreat to kickstart a writing routine – a set number of hours you will write per day / week, for example. Aim to keep a schedule which will be achievable but will also represent an achievement.

VISIT AN
UNUSUAL
LANDSCAPE

Past the village of Armoy, in Northern Ireland's County Antrim, ordinary countryside turns into a gateway to another world when the 'dark hedges' suddenly appear at the roadside. Taking in the long row of brooding, intertwined trees, it's not hard to imagine this was a landscape that inspired C.S. Lewis and his Chronicles of Narnia.

Plan your trip to a similarly startling landscape. Stay awhile, and afterwards:

> Write something inspired by your visit – be it a short story, a lyric, or an outline of a new novel.

> Scour a map for evocative place names. Write a poem or dialogue inspired by one (or more) of these.

Create a map for your novel. Where do the major events take place? What is the landscape for your novel? Can you heighten and intensify the atmosphere and mood of the novel by the landscape you have created? Make notes as you work, and pinpoint specific scenes in which you can apply your new insights.

SPREAD OUT
WITH THE
NEWSPAPERS

Afterwards:

Make notes on what would have been making the
international news during the events of your novel.

And the national news?

Complete your note-taking with a survey of what
appeared in your protagonist's local news. What would
they have read on the billboard outside their local
newsagents? What would have hijacked their attention
online?

Pick one of these news events to develop into a news
story that unfolds during the course of your novel.
Create a timeline showing how the story intersects
with that of your novel.

As well as giving potentially useful dramatic and moral parallels to your central story, and helping you to think about the wider context of your novel, this exercise will help you pay attention to your timeline. It's crucial that you have a clear timeline, and ideally a sense of urgency, to the events of your novel. We need to hear the clock ticking.

You might:

> Pick an important day in the events of the novel and write a page for a newspaper which would have appeared on that day.

> Work a fragment or refrain from one of the articles into your novel draft.

RUN

Haruki Murakami assimilated long-distance running into his writing life, consciously making it an essential part of his new lifestyle as a serious novelist. Running exercised his ability for keeping pace. He had to leave each run with the ability and desire to run more the next day – as he did with novel writing. Running gave him solitude – a writer's space, and – importantly – kept him in motion each day to counter all those hours spent at a desk.

Afterwards:

> Read Murakami's *What I Talk About When I Talk About Running* – reflections on his life as a runner and novelist.

You might also:

> Write an essay on an element of your writing life. The exercise might lead to ideas for the marketing of your work, an interesting piece of writing in itself you may seek to publish, or help you to consider how your daily life can better support your writing.

Your aim is to find a writing rhythm that you are comfortable with – one that allows you to keep going.

TAKE A RIVERSIDE WALK

Reflect on the passage of time in your novel. Think about the internal timeline of your draft – the changing seasons, the passing days, the years mounting imperceptibly like a pile of autumn leaves. A river can remain unchanging through the years and seasons – only perhaps the faintest trace of time in some ancient graffiti or fleeting wildlife. Think of your novel, and the tells of time passing – sometimes quiet like those of the river, sometimes with the bombast of fireworks or sirens.

Afterwards:

> Write a scene containing one of your novel's key themes, in which your protagonist appears as a child or in their dotage.

> Plot out your novel's timeline – confirming it is consistent and robust. Note where you show the passing seasons and years, and where you can add to this.

You might also:

> List as many different points at which you could enter
> the novel's timeline as possible.

There may be an option you have overlooked which could add greater momentum or originality to the narrative. Even if you determine to keep things as they are, considering the range of possibilities can prod you to make greater use of your novel's extended timeline, including what you currently consider as backstory. For example, a period of crisis or trauma only briefly mentioned in a current draft may emerge as a more fully developed scene you decide you must find a spot for somewhere in your novel; or a detail of family history might suggest an entirely new slant to your narrative.

TAKE A VOW
OF SILENCE

Pick somewhere with plenty of conversation around you – an airport holding area, a train at rush hour, a bustling café. Listen – making note of any conversations or lines that frustrate you, as well as any that intrigue.

Frustrated or bored by what you hear? Likely too much information, likely plenty of repetition too. Or perhaps a mundane conversation about what's for tea or who's meeting where and at what time.

Intrigued? Well, something that stands out; perhaps something you have to guess the meaning of. A surprising or beautiful turn of phrase. Perhaps just a few snippets of language interest you from the torrent of words around you.

Later:

> Look again at one of the snippets you felt worth saving. Without thinking too much, can you construct a quick character around these words?

Do the same for one of the conversations you'd happily forget.

You may find that by exaggerating the awfulness of the boring dialogue you are able to come up with a memorable character, but I'd wager it was easier to construct a character from the intriguing dialogue. It's the peculiarities of spoken language that can powerfully convey character, whilst generalized or clichéd dialogue can leave a frustratingly vague sense of character. These are the lines that could be spoken by anybody, where you are aiming for a reader to be able to pick out any line of dialogue in your prose and know who has spoken.

Next:

Take out your novel draft. Is every line of dialogue one that would make your cut? Do you sometimes include information you feel the reader needs to know, which could be better expressed in the main text – or perhaps isn't needed at all? Do you sometimes repeat yourself? Look out for repetitions in dialogue, but also where you repeat information already covered in dialogue in the main text or vice versa. Do you sometimes allow your characters to talk in cliché, or simply say too much? Often less dialogue is necessary than you might at first think.

When writing fresh dialogue, think about:

Leaving room for interpretation

Conveying character through dialogue

You will also be able to add your own pointers from your writer's date. For example, you may have found that dialogue that stuck with you had an unusual word order, and decide to experiment with this in your own dialogue. Or it may have been fragments of a foreign tongue that spoke to you from the clamor of voices. Again, see if you can work with this in your writing.

 Roddy Doyle's slim *Two Pints* is set in a Belfast bar and written entirely in dialogue.

GO TO THE
BEACH

Contemplate the key themes of your novel whilst soaking up the colours, elements and open space of the beach… and afterwards:

> Block out the environment / 'map' of your novel,
> making note of the dominant colours, theme and mood
> in each new location.

Sometimes, to breathe new life into a scene, you might need to take your character out of familiar surroundings. To investigate this:

> Rewrite one of your novel's key scenes in a fresh
> location. Before you write, remind yourself of the
> central mood and key theme you wish to convey, and
> use this to guide you in selecting your new location.

You might also:

> Write a message in a bottle on behalf of one of your
> characters.

VISIT A CASTLE

Soak up the atmosphere and focus your thoughts on the castle's history, particularly the sieges, threats, and attacks it may have weathered over the years. Afterwards:

> Create a mindmap of as many of the threats the castle has faced as possible – from the time of construction right up to the present.

Next, consider your novel, and the threats faced by your central character(s).

> Brainstorm as many ways to intensify or multiply these as you can. Make notes on how resilient your character is to each threat, and if / when they might ultimately succumb to each one.

> Pick a colour to highlight the threats that form the core of your story.

Pick a colour to highlight those threats that are useful to parallel and give resonance to the core narrative, but which will play a secondary role in your story.

Those threats that are left over will not feature in your novel, though you might find they inform your writing in unexpected ways. (For example, you may have decided on a physical weakness which will affect your character long after the events of the novel are closed – simply knowing this may subtly alter your description and handling of your character.) Return to work on your draft with fresh insight and spend some time implementing any required developments.

GO HOUSE HUNTING

Complete a sketch or collage of the homes of three of your characters. Be sure to make each stand out from the others, and to convey as much of your character as possible in the home they have made.

Afterwards:

Let your mind wander over the three dwellings you have worked on. Pick an object from one of the dwellings that could play a significant part in your plotline. Draw and / or describe the object. Make notes on its potential relevance to the plot.

Focus in on one of the rooms / areas you have drawn. Spend some time thinking about what might take place there. General happenings plus one key dramatic incident. Make notes on this.

> Have your protagonist write a letter introducing
> himself and his home to a stranger (e.g. a couch surfer
> / exchange student / distant family member) who
> is coming to stay. He must introduce the principal
> characters of the novel, as well as himself, in the letter.

This last exercise is a good way of finding your character's voice, and of testing out writing your narrative in the first person if this is something you are considering. It might even influence the way you decide to tell your story – such as through a series of letters, or diary entries. Or perhaps the candid or confessional tone of letter writing is something you will want simply to keep in mind as you write.

If you are in the early stages of developing your novel, or are looking to make a radical change to your novel, it's worth pausing here to:

> Brainstorm as many different forms in which you might
> write your novel as possible. For example, you might
> write your novel as a series of letters, or diary entries, or
> through the voice of your second lead character rather
> than your protagonist.

 See Date 51: Listen to a Professional Storyteller

FEED THE DUCKS OR GO WILDLIFE SPOTTING

Afterwards:

Re-write one of your novel's key scenes, replacing your characters with the ducks or other wildlife you observed.

Give each of your characters one or more qualities from the ducks or other wildlife you observed. Revise or rewrite another of your novel's key scenes with these qualities in mind.

You might also:

> Rewrite a key dialogue in your novel to take place
> whilst your characters are feeding the ducks / wildlife
> spotting. Look for ways in which the action or setting
> mirrors or contrasts with the topic of conversation.

Giving your dialogue a strong counterpoint like this allows you to experiment with subtext – loading your characters' words with meaning without directly stating their thoughts or feelings. You might use this technique to revitalize any sections of dialogue you are not fully satisfied with in your novel draft.

RIDE A TANDEM

Pay attention to how you begin, how you find a pace and any wobbly moments! At some point during the ride, switch places. Afterwards:

> Pick one of your protagonist's key relationships. Can you heighten / intensify it? Pinpoint any new places where this second character can play an active role in the plot – where they can have greater impact on your narrative.

> Tell the story from the Point of View of this second character. Where does his / her version of events differ from that of your protagonist?

Use this exercise to help you discover unexplored conflict within the narrative, even where two characters are supposedly working together and as 'in synch' as the riders of a tandem bicycle.

35/52

TAKE YOUR WRITING OUTSIDE

Make sure you've plenty of time, and simply take your writing outside. Just a pencil and something to make notes on is all you need. Think about your novel's biggest problem. That bit that needs fixing but you've never got round to. Make a start.

Stuck?

Think about your protagonist's biggest problem. What are they trying to reach, or solve, through the novel? What's getting in their way? Can you make their problem harder, the obstacles larger?

How will your character meet this renewed challenge?

Will they become tougher, more ingenious? Note down the new action they will take.

Return to your manuscript's problem.

Keep going.

 See Date 40: Attend an Opening

FIND YOUR WAY OUT OF A MAZE OR LABYRINTH

Afterwards, think about your novel as a maze: where do you lead your reader to a dead end, and do you offer enough potential paths through the narrative to offer your reader a satisfying experience?

Next:

> Map out the alternative outcomes to your novel in the form of a maze.

You can use your maze to think through the different outcomes – even testing out some of the different ones – in order to check you have the best ending for your novel.

> Add detail to your maze, signposting where a different
> action or decision on behalf of your characters could
> have resulted in a different outcome.

You may find that a small action or decision is all that tips the balance towards the novel's outcome, or you may find a number of points where the outcome becomes increasingly difficult to avoid. Analyze those decisions or actions – you may find your protagonist's fatal flaw here, for example. It's worth noting where in the manuscript these occur. Was the ending always in the beginning – determined by some course of action your character took early on? Or does your character have the opportunity to change the novel's outcome until much later in the novel?

If your maze doesn't push you on past your novel's current ending, address this and make notes on the implications of such a change.

 See Example Texts

VISIT YOUR FAVOURITE CAFÉ

Before you go:

> Write down everything you know – as much as you can remember – about the place.

At the café:

> Add to your notes.

How accurate was your original description? Was there anything new to add? Anything specific to the day of your visit? Next:

> Pick one of your characters and write a description of the café from their Point of View. What would they notice? What would they leave out? What kind of language would they use?

Pick a different character and do the same. How will the description change when written from the second character's perspective?

The differences between your two characters' café accounts may be subtle or pronounced – but they are crucial. You could repeat this exercise in a variety of familiar locations, to improve your memory and observational skills, as well as your mastery of Point of View.

 See Date 51: Listen to a Professional Storyteller

INDULGE YOUR BIGGEST PASSION

Sometimes, no matter how much we try to poke, prod and worry a revision into life, it remains resolutely flat. This is the point at which to return to your own biggest passion. Your passion should revive flagging spirits, nourish your creativity and – like Ernest Hemingway's devotion to bullfighting and fishing, and Haruki Murakami's dual loves of music and running – may even turn out to have a remarkable influence on your writing.

Afterwards, in a free-writing exercise:

Write something inspired by your passion.

Next:

Reflect on your protagonist's passions. Ardent desire is a spur to action, and so intensifying your character's passion can add vigour to their actions.

Write or revise one of your novel's key scenes using the lexicon of your character's passion. (If necessary, research your character's passion, so you are familiar with any specialist terminology.)

You may not use this scene in its entirety, but a layer of metaphor or simile stemming from your character's passion can help lift your prose, and tighten the novel's Point of View.

FOLLOW EVERY IMPULSE YOU HAVE

Set yourself a time limit to indulge every whim and desire. We constantly edit our thoughts and desires but for the duration of the task, allow yourself no second guessing. Afterwards:

> Write about a character who acts without conscience; a character whose actions may shock and horrify a reader – and who may not be at all likeable.

Next:

> Think about your protagonist's actions through the course of the novel. Does your protagonist always act reasonably? Is there a danger you are making your character too nice? Too predictable? Make notes

on where you might address this if so. Ask the same
questions of the other characters in your novel, before
returning to your draft.

ATTEND AN OPENING

Pick something you wouldn't normally attend, something new and different.

Afterwards, reflect on your experience. Did you feel there were any barriers to attendance – special clothes, or particular social skills needed, for example – or were you simply welcomed in and enveloped in a new world? Was there anything that alienated you, as a newcomer to this particular event / society?

It's important to remember that when you ask any reader to enter your novel, you are inviting them to enter a unique world that you have created. Whilst easiest to understand in relation to a writer of fantasy fiction, in which a world may be extremely different from the physical world the reader inhabits, this is true of any writer – even if you feel you are simply presenting the world as you see it.

Therefore, you must extend courtesy to your readers – in ushering them into the world of your novel, making no assumptions as author on their world view (this includes not dressing up your own opinion as that of one or more of your characters), and valuing their time and attention such that not a word in your novel is wasted, or without meaning.

> Revisit anything in your novel you have reason to believe may make a reader uncomfortable. Interrogate whether it is justified in terms of your novel (keeping it if it is), or simply represents your own world view. This includes stereotypes, prejudices, and assumptions that are too narrow. To help you do this, imagine a reader from a culture very different to yours reading your novel.

If you can help someone who wouldn't usually read a novel in your genre to appreciate your novel, you will increase your chances of attracting the widest possible readership. This is also true of the world you have chosen for your story. It doesn't mean diluting your ideas, but keeping in mind the idea of courtesy towards your reader – whoever they may be.

To bring this theme into your writing:

> Plan or write a scene in which one of your characters appears somewhere they clearly do not belong. Somewhere they feel 'out of place'.

You might also:

> Make a list of objections a publisher / agent / reader might make to investing in your novel. For example, a setting that may have limited appeal; an unclear target readership; characters with names your reader might struggle to pronounce.

Answer those objections! Will that unappealing setting be so fully realized it becomes a strength? Can you make a clear decision on target readership, seeking advice if necessary? Is your character so memorable that the cumbersome name fits him perfectly?

Continue your draft only when you are satisfied you have faced the potential objections to your novel, and are confident in overcoming these.

 See Date 35: Take Your Writing Outside, if you need some help here.

 See Date 41: Embrace Something You Dislike

EMBRACE SOMETHING YOU DISLIKE

In real life, people can be stubborn, static and frustratingly resistant to change. Many of us would not make terribly interesting characters in a novel. But the personal transformation involved in something as small as eating a delicacy you have avoided since childhood, or casting off a long-held prejudice against a sport or pastime can alter that – reminding us that *in fiction, characters need to demonstrate the capacity to change*. If they did not, readers would not be very interested in following their struggles.

Think of a point in your novel where your central character demonstrates a capacity for change.

Sketch out a scene – inspired by your own experience of embracing something you dislike – in which this

ability for your character to transform his- or herself
is glimpsed.

Since it is never possible to assume each individual reader shares
your worldview, preferences or opinions, it is also valuable (and
wise) to challenge these during the course of writing or revising
a novel. To help you do this:

> Pick one of your novel's key ideas and research the
> opposite point of view. Suspend your opinion, and
> really get stuck in here.

> Find somewhere for the opposite argument to live in
> your novel, if it is not already there.

The aim is not to dilute your ideas, but to ensure you are not
writing from too narrow a perspective.

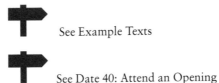

See Example Texts

See Date 40: Attend an Opening

GO PEOPLE WATCHING

Pick somewhere busy – such as a shopping centre or a park – somewhere you can watch people come and go. Notice the rhythms of movement around you – the groupings, the individuals intersecting other groups or walkers – as well as the gestures and movements of individuals.

That park, for instance, might remind you how children and young adults can appear to be almost constantly in motion. How static the accompanying adults can seem!

Afterwards:

> Pick one of the scenes in your novel in which a number of people are present.
>
> Rework the scene, paying attention to the bodies and their movements.
>
> You can extend this approach to further sections of your novel.

GATECRASH

You might crash an art opening, film premiere or industry function if you're feeling brave; or simply tag along to the leaving party of someone you don't know very well. Escape your comfort zone, and then get tough on your central characters. Place them in awkward situations and have them squirm. Embarrass them. To warm up:

> Write a scene in which your character turns up somewhere uninvited.

> Write a scene in which one of your characters loses their dignity.

Then:

> Write a list of the main challenges your protagonist faces, and note how he/ she overcomes those challenges. Brainstorm ways of making the situation 10 times more awkward. Then 20. Write one of those scenes.

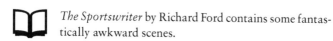 *The Sportswriter* by Richard Ford contains some fantastically awkward scenes.

VISIT A HALL OF MIRRORS

Make a sketch of, or notes on, the different features that stand out in each likeness of yourself and afterwards, inspired by this:

> Create a series of sketches of your central character –
> each one exaggerating or stretching certain features in
> the same way a hall of mirrors does.

You might use an idea sparked by your sketches to add something remarkable to your character's appearance; you might also allow the distorted features to suggest a focus on an aspect of the character's personality. To help you do this:

> Assign each sketch to one of the characters in your
> novel, so that the different sketches represent the
> different ways in which the surrounding characters view
> your protagonist. If the protagonist's brother thinks

he is greedy and materialistic, for example, this might be represented by an exaggeratedly wide girth or the jowls of a particularly well-fed dog. Your protagonist's preoccupation with a perceived imperfection such as a too large nose or too small ears might also show itself in your hall of mirrors.

Afterwards, look back at your draft with a heightened sensitivity to the different ways your character is perceived by others, as well as him- or herself. Revise or write fresh material where necessary. You might also:

> Write a scene in which one of your characters looks in a mirror.

 See Example Texts

WATCH THE WEATHER

For a full week, write nothing but a weather diary. Try to be as accurate as possible in describing the day's weather, using vocabulary that is varied and evocative. After the week is up:

Write or rewrite a scene or moment in which the weather reflects your protagonist's mood.

Write or rewrite a scene or moment in which the weather is in stark contrast to your protagonist's mood.

Write or rewrite a scene or moment in which the weather causes a major conflict.

Choose one or more of the above scenes. Revise the scene, so that references to the weather are figurative rather than literal – intensifying the mood / atmosphere. You can be as radical as you would like in this. For example, weather might be used as a metaphor, or you might take out all references to the weather so that only a heightened mood is left.

You might return to this date in a different season.

DO SOMETHING TO GET YOUR ADRENALINE GOING

Novels that connect with readers are based on authentic emotion. All of the dates in this book are designed to help you be the kind of writer who is not afraid to look inwards in order to write. It takes courage to show up on the page – to realize that as a writer you will be exposed to scrutiny, and that in dealing with any difficult or taboo subject as much good fiction does, some readers may ask how close the fiction you have created is to your life.

And so, as in life, there is a strong drive for the writer to cover or lighten unpalatable emotion such as shame, fear, grief or desire. Even a writer who embraces these themes will often present an approximation or imitation of a difficult emotion rather than looking within, and even a writer who is able to look within will often find the emotion squirming away, turning into something subtly different, anything so as not to show up on the page.

To begin work on this (and it is something I believe a writer never stops needing to work on):

Embrace your feelings before, during, and after completing your writer's date. Write them down, as accurately as possible.

Find somewhere in your novel to include these feelings. Work hard on bringing the authenticity of the emotion to your novel.

Write a few lines on why writing this story is so important to you. Try to pin down the originating emotion – did you begin to write because something made you angry or sad or afraid?

Next, note down the one most important thing you want your reader to take away from the story.

Consider your plot outline (looking at a synopsis if you have already prepared one), and rewrite it in terms of the emotional journey of your characters. Where you are inviting a reader to experience a different emotion to your characters, note this too. Try to align this with your stated intention for your novel – what your reader must take from it.

Make sure you are attuned to the emotional core of your novel. If this aspect of the novel has been neglected in favour of a different element – such as strong pacing, or developing an exciting and complex plot, for example – bring it back into focus, and the novel back into balance.

DANCE

Dance with others or alone, salsa dance or freestyle. Dance for *at least twenty minutes* – and continue for as long as you would like.

Afterwards:

Describe what is unique about the way three of your characters move.

Describe the physical strengths and weaknesses of three of your characters.

Write a scene in which one of your characters dances.

Write a scene in which one of your characters undertakes a physical challenge.

IMMERSE YOURSELF IN A DIFFERENT LANGUAGE

Perhaps a language you know already, perhaps one you've always been interested in, perhaps one that laps at your novel's edges. A spoken language, a lost language or a silent language such as sign or Braille – whichever you choose, relish the opportunity to explore a different way of communicating. This short hiatus from the dominant tongue of your novel can allow you to realize a subculture more fully, or give you a sharper ear for the language you choose.

Afterwards:

> Decide upon the five most important words in your novel, and write them down – in the language of your novel and the second language you have chosen.

Create a mindmap detailing the associations of each of these key words, and showing where they interconnect.

Put it somewhere you can see it often as you write.

You might also:

Research the etymology of each word to spark further ideas.

These five words and their associations will likely lead you to your novel's key themes, and provide fresh ideas of how you can weave these into your novel. Having a well-developed sense of your novel's underlying themes makes it easier to write and revise your material. This is because knowing what you want to convey can feed into choices such as what to describe and how.

 See Example Texts

MEDITATE

Novel writing can deplete your physical and mental reserves, so it is essential to treat yourself kindly. Meditation is one method you can use to keep your consciousness scrubbed clean. Practicing mindfulness can also help you to avoid some of the myriad saboteurs that face any artist. One of the worst is allowing your own writing time to be sacrificed in favour of trivial temptations. You'll know the ones that most often sabotage you and your writing. The phonecall you should have let the answerphone pick up; checking one of your multiple in-boxes; succumbing to five minutes on a social networking site; compulsive snacking to sweeten the graft. Meditation can help still your mind and allow you to see your true goals with greater clarity and conviction. Afterwards:

> Decide on a clear policy for protecting your writing time, and tell those closest to you. For example, 'I will not answer the phone when it is my writing time. / One Saturday a month I will not be available as I will be writing.'

When you have precious time to write, allow no one and nothing to sabotage this.

WATCH A BUSKER PERFORM

Linger to enjoy the ambience, paying attention until a scene (and person) you may have paid scant attention to takes centre stage.

Afterwards:

Take one of your secondary or minor characters and write a detailed physical description of them. Follow them home. Who and what do you find there?

Brainstorm ways to extend or enrich this character's role in your novel.

Write or rewrite a scene in which this character's significance to the novel is amplified.

 See Example Texts

LISTEN TO A PROFESSIONAL STORYTELLER

Stories are all around us, but the ancient art of storytelling is a communication between storyteller and audience, without print or technology. Indeed, a traditional storyteller does not work from a script but learns both the shape of the story (using, for example, the key events, sounds patterns, phrasing and repetitions) and its emotional dynamics, presenting it anew with each telling.

There's a pleasing freedom and flexibility of form that novelists can make use of too, which stems from knowing the foundations of a story scrupulously well. For, although much of the novelist's endeavour is to nail down the story – the order in which it is told, the precise words with which it is given life – that story can then be retold in a thousand ways. Think of your reader retelling your story; each would begin with a different thread and enter and leave the narrative at a different point.

This is why, like the traditional storyteller, you must have hammered at and tested out each different plot strand until you know your story so well you could tell it in a myriad of different ways. So, for an interval, forget the structure you have determined for your novel, and:

Retell the story from the perspective of the second most important character.

Retell the story from the perspective of the principal antagonist.

Retell the story from the perspective of one of the minor characters.

Retell the story, focusing on its subplot. (If there is more than one subplot, repeat.)

Tell the story from 2/3rds of the way through to the end.

Tell the story backwards. (This allows you to focus on making your story fit its conclusion, and whatever it is you want the reader to take away from the novel.)

Find another way to tell your story.

Each of these retellings gives you the chance to interrogate your plot, and add complexity, focus and clarification where needed.

Afterwards, you can incorporate any changes into your 'true' plotline, where, just as with the professional storyteller, *who* is telling the story comes into sharp focus.

If you have chosen to write a first-person narrative, you must make sure you position your Point of View character so as to access as much of the action as possible, and find solutions for those parts of the story at which that character cannot be present.

If you are using an omniscient narrator, you must still be aware that you must tell each part of the story from a clear perspective. It can't be everyone's story simultaneously, so you must choose whose story you are telling. There's a temptation to jump from character to character, as after all one reason for choosing to write with an omniscient narrator is to be 'all-seeing' – able to hover godlike over the world you have created and reveal whatever is necessary to the reader. Whilst there is certainly more liberty to show the perspectives and thoughts of different characters in a straightforward manner in this form, moving from one Point of View to another without a clear reason to do so, and without consideration of the reader's experience so that they are hardly able to 'catch up' with one character before you jump to another, can be a symptom of an uncontrolled draft.

Whilst writing from a first person narrator or an omniscient narrator are the two most commonly used forms, it is also of course possible to experiment with form such as writing from multiple first person narrators, or using a hybrid between the omniscient narrator and first person, for example.

Whichever form you ultimately decide on, mastering Point of View is essential. This comes in never failing to remember whose perspective you are writing from, and knowing that character intimately so that their hopes, fears, dreams, past and present are contained in the very words you use to tell their story.

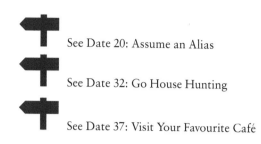

See Date 20: Assume an Alias

See Date 32: Go House Hunting

See Date 37: Visit Your Favourite Café

PLAY

Whilst all of the tasks in this book require a spirit of playfulness and exploration, the willingness and capacity to play is so crucial to any creative act, that this last writer's date is simply an invitation to play in any way you choose.

Play, and keep playing.

To remind you to do this:

> Write a list of as many activities as possible that you
> would consider 'play'. Put this list somewhere you can
> see it often.

It's vital to keep a healthy reserve of playfulness, for it is the flow of play – so abundant in early childhood – which allows us to experiment, to push the boundaries, to avoid closing down our ideas too early, and to get down to the serious business of completing a novel.

ON EDITING

Whilst many of the 52 dates in this book will help you in the development or revision of your draft, a number will also support you in editing your material.

It's important to remember, however, that whilst improving your editing skills will improve your draft, becoming too concerned with editing too early can cause you to shut down your ideas before they are fully developed, or slow you down so that the end of the novel becomes unattainable.

Every writer works differently, and it is simply a matter of paying attention to what works for you – you might feel comfortable with a high degree of editing as you write your draft, or with getting a full draft down before paring it back in a later editing period.

Editing is, of course, as much of a skill and an art as writing. Structural editing takes on board the re-organisation of plot, which can become extremely complex. This is one reason why, if possible, it can work better to commit development time earlier on in the process. A more straightforward copyedit can take place once the central facets of the novel are more or less in place.

Here, the focus is on the surface of the writing – the specific words chosen to present the ideas, characters, happenings and world of the novel. The requirements of each text will be unique, but here are some general thoughts on editing, some of which may apply to your draft.

A manuscript can harbor a great deal of unintentional repetition – from using the same word too many times in close proximity, to repeating information from one scene to the next, to using dialogue to reiterate what main text has already said. Readers have limited patience for repetition, so something will have to go. (Of course, sometimes repetition can be used to strong effect – in building up resonance, or showing how different characters view the same event, for example. It is unintentional repetition that must always be interrogated.)

Good writing rises above clichéd phrasing. It is hard to demonstrate a unique voice and style if you are using bland, well-worn phrasing.

Sometimes a really strong line will be striking the same note as other material, and will have to go.

Aim for the most impact in the fewest words. In practice, this means you need to have a surplus of strong material. A happy scenario is the editing of a good draft of 100,000 words down to an excellent novel of 80,000 words. Once you start paring each sentence down to its essentials, you will discover more and more inessential words. For example, when recounting events in chronological order, the words 'then' or 'next' are often not needed. Dialogue can often be stripped back a great deal: 'I think we need to...' can become 'we need to...'; 'you must work hard' can become 'work hard'.

You may have dwelt too long on minor gestures, and need to pare these back in order to regain the focus of the piece. Like many editorial considerations, it can be hard for a writer to see this too close to the time of writing, which is why the advice is often to 'put a text away' for a period of time before editing, or to have someone else undertake the editing for you.

Material that is overly sentimental will usually need paring back.

Give strong consideration to cutting any material which tells the reader what to think.

Give strong consideration to cutting 'domestic' material – phone calls, arrangements being made for meetings, the making of plans. The tension is often lost at these points. The reader can fill these bits in. Instead of hearing a plan being made, then witnessing it in action, most often it is far stronger for the reader simply to witness it in action. Phone calls often cause a dip in the novel's tension and contain too much 'padding' – material the novel could do equally well without.

Weaker material must go. Sometimes you'll find the story can be told as well without it; sometimes you'll find you have covered the same material in a better way elsewhere; sometimes you'll need to write some replacement text.

Ensure consistency of tense is maintained.

Ensure the novel's Point of View is tightly controlled. It's easy to drop out of a character's perspective without intending to through the course of a novel.

It's worth keeping an 'editorial style sheet', recording preferences where there is more than one choice of spelling or anything in the way you have presented your material that you need to remember. If it helps to keep a note of tense or Point of View here, do. The earlier in the process you put this together and the more thorough you are, the less time consuming a final proofread / edit will be.

Editing on-screen can allow you to make use of features such as Word's 'find' function to weed out inconsistent spellings or check your suspicions on words you have overused through the manuscript. However, always work from a printed version after this, as it is easier to spot error, and areas for improvement.

You might try:

Taking a section of your manuscript of roughly 100 words, and editing it down to 80 words – then 50.

6 EXAMPLES

1

'We were drinking lemonade and ice, in the old green ragged scout tent, side by side on two grey-brown army surplus beds.'
>
'We were drinking lemonade and ice in the ragged green scout tent, side by side on two army surplus beds.'

First version contains too many adjectives to picture scene clearly enough.

2

'I steadied him on the side of the bed and gave him some water, which he struggled to drink, spilling it down his chin like a baby.'
>
'I steadied him on the side of the bed and gave him some water, which he spilled down his chin like a baby.'

If he spills his drink, he is clearly struggling with it, so we can cut the first version down.

3

'I helped him to a small wooden chair, changed the
sheets, changed his clothes, sponged the floor and
helped him back into bed.'

>

*'hauled him back into bed,' would provide a more
precise and evocative word choice.*

4

'I didn't remind him of the simple fact we had sold
his house.'

>

'I didn't remind him we had sold his house.'

Same meaning, fewer words.

5

'Heaving ajar the heavy paneled door'

>

'Heaving ajar the paneled door'

*'Heaving' implies 'heavy'. Let the more powerful
word do the work.*

fewer words.

'Charlie jerked out of his daydream and a couple of seconds later nearly jumped out of his skin at the sound of a bottle shattering against the window-sill.'

>

'Charlie jerked out of his daydream and a couple of seconds later nearly jumped out of his skin at the sound of something shattering against the window-sill.'

We can't assume Charlie knows what the sound is. This is an example of the writer telling us a fact and forgetting to show the events of the novel as the Point of View character experiences it. Will he even be able to locate the sound so precisely?

 New Hart's Rules: The Handbook of Style for Writers and Editors and *New Oxford Dictionary for Writers and Editors: The Essential A-Z Guide to the Written Word* are two handy reference books to help you tackle matters of grammar, spelling, and presentation.

EXAMPLE TEXTS

2
GO GEOCACHING

The Girl with the Dragon Tattoo

Prologue
Mystery of the birthday flowers – identity of
sender and 82-year-old recipient unknown.

Chapter 1
The lost trial of journalist Karl Mikael
Blomkvist against financier Hans-Erik
Wennerström – but why did an experienced
journalist make such an error?

Lifelong enmity with former journalist William
Borg introduced. Borg now works in PR; links to
Wennerström.

Old schoolfriend, Robert Lindberg introduced
– he planted the ill-fated story with Blomkvist.

Chapter 2
Meet Dragan Armansky, CEO of Milton
Security.

Meet Lisbeth Salander, unlikely private investigator. What is the secret that makes Armansky wary of her, despite her talent and his regard for her?

Salander hired to look into the Blomkvist case – she suspects a set-up.

Chapter 4
Bromkvist receives a strange invitation – to meet the retired industrialist Henrik Vanger.

Vanger proposes to engage Bromkvist to write a history of his family, and discover who killed 16-year-old Harriet Vanger.

 Back to Date

3
ATTEND A
CELEBRITY APPEARANCE

Atonement – Robbie: cleaning lady's son, graduates with the top mark in his year at Cambridge; vs a disappointing third-class degree for Cecilia, daughter of his sponsor and mother's employer (note that her degree is not even 'official' and is a cause of dissent in the household) – much to unpack in these 2 seemingly small details...

The Great Gatsby – The excessively wealthy Jay Gatsby exhibits a romanticism unlike anyone the narrator has ever met before. Tom Buchanan has a rare sporting accolade to his name.

Harry Potter and the Philosopher's Stone – As an infant, Harry survived an attack that left his parents dead, saw off Voldemort – a wizard so evil that many will not speak his name – and was left with a scar like a bolt of lightening. He is famous in the wizarding world, although growing up among 'muggles', he does not know this until his eleventh birthday.

 Back to Date

4
ATTEND A TWO-TEAM SPORTS FIXTURE

Harry Potter vs Draco Malfoy in *Harry Potter and the Philosopher's Stone*

Round 1: train to Hogwarts
Harry snubs Malfoy's offer of friendship.
Malfoy insults Harry's friends.
Harry and Ron stand up to Malfoy and his friends Crabbe and Goyle.

Goyle tries to steal Harry's chocolate frog.
Ron's rat sees them off.
Match to: Harry

Round 2: flying lesson
Harry and Malfoy are now members of two
opposing school houses, Gryffindor and Slytherin.
When one of Harry's housemates falls from his
broomstick and is taken to the hospital wing,
Malfoy sneers and snatches away the magic ball
his gran has just sent him.
Harry challenges Malfoy and discovers he can
ride a broomstick – without ever being taught!
Professor McGonagall appears, furious at Harry,
but also impressed by his talent.
He will become the youngest house quidditch
player in about a century.
Malfoy taunts him again, and challenges him to
a midnight wizard's duel. Ron will be Harry's
second.
It was a trick! Ron, Harry and Hermione
narrowly escape being caught by the professors
and end up in the forbidden corridor, where they
meet a monstrous dog with three heads.
Match to: Malfoy

 Back to Date

22
BROWSE A FLEA MARKET
OR CAR BOOT SALE

The vase in *Atonement* is of great symbolic importance to the Tallis family, and of dramatic important when it is smashed in a quarrel between Cecelia and Briony, causing Cecelia to jump into the fountain in her underwear. Marries plot and theme seamlessly.

 Back to Date

36
FIND YOUR WAY OUT OF
A MAZE OR LABYRINTH

Each entry below shows how the plot develops at the beginning of *Atonement*. The first item of each entry is the 'correct' path through the novel, and alternative outcomes are marked >. Where there is more than one alternative outcome suggested, these are marked OR.

Cecilia quarrels with childhood friend Robbie, the cleaning lady's son.
In their quarrel, a priceless vase is smashed over a fountain. Cecilia strips to her underwear to retrieve it.

> Only to find...

> Cecilia's father continues to sponsor his education and Robbie achieves his ambition and returns for Cecilia.

> Despite realizing he is in love, Robbie decides first to complete his medicine degree.

1. Cecilia quarrels with childhood friend Robbie, the cleaning lady's son.

2. In their quarrel, a priceless vase is smashed over a fountain. Cecilia strips to her underwear to retrieve it.

3. Robbie writes a letter declaring his love for Cecilia.

4. Cecilia's brother Leon visits, bringing his friend, Paul Marshall. He invites Robbie to dinner.

> Robbie refuses an invitation to dinner.

OR > Leon obliges Cecilia's request to retract Robbie's invitation to dinner.

> Snubbed, Robbie leaves home and refuses further sponsorship from Cecilia's father.

> Instead, he ...

5. Robbie chances upon Cecilia's younger sister Briony and asks her to deliver his letter.

> Briony tells him to do it himself.

13. Briony searches alone and discovers Lola outside the island temple in the dark, attacked by a man. Neither see his face, but Briony convinces her cousin it was Robbie.

14. Robbie is accused of molesting a young girl, and at once loses Cecilia and her father's sponsorship; his freedom and future.

6. Robbie realizes it is an early draft of the letter – crudely stating his desire.

...obbie and ...ilia search ...ether, and ...tinue their ...macy.

12. Robbie goes off on his own

7. Briony reads the letter before delivering it.

> And tells her sister.

> Who feigns disgust and makes plans to...

OR > And tells her mother.

> Who rips it up.

...the mother ...kes sure ...e of the ...dren are ...on their ...

> The ...her calls ...police

11. The family splits up to go and look for them.

10. In the middle of a disastrous dinner, twins Pierrot and Jackson run away.

9. Briony walks in on a moment of passion between Robbie and Cecilia.

8. And tells her cousin Lola.

> In the middle of a disastrous dinner, Briony blurts out what she has seen.

> Briony runs away.

Robbie writes a letter declaring his love for
Cecilia. > Despite realizing he is in love, Robbie
decides first to complete his medicine degree. >
Cecilia's father continues to sponsor his
education and Robbie achieves his ambition and
returns for Cecilia > Only to find...
Cecilia's brother Leon visits, bringing his friend,
Paul Marshall. He invites Robbie to dinner. >
Robbie refuses an invitation to dinner. OR >
Leon obliges Cecilia's request to retract Robbie's
invitation to dinner. > Snubbed, Robbie leaves
home and refuses further sponsorship from
Cecilia's father. Instead, he...
Robbie chances upon Cecilia's younger sister
Briony and asks her to deliver his letter. >
Briony tells him to do it himself.
Robbie realizes it is an early draft of the letter
– crudely stating his desire.
Briony reads the letter before delivering it. >
And tells her sister. > Who feigns disgust and
makes plans to... OR > And tells her mother. >
Who rips it up.
And tells her cousin Lola.
Briony walks in on a moment of passion between
Robbie and Cecilia. > Briony runs away.
In the middle of a disastrous dinner, twins
Pierrot and Jackson run away. > In the middle of
a disastrous dinner, Briony blurts out what she
has seen.
The family splits up to go and look for the
missing children. > The mother makes sure
none of the children are left on their own. OR >
The mother calls the police.

Robbie goes off on his own. > Robbie and
Cecilia search together, and continue their
intimacy.
Briony searches alone and discovers Lola outside
the island temple in the dark, attacked by a man.
Neither see his face, but Briony convinces her
cousin it was Robbie.
Robbie is accused of molesting a young girl, and
at once loses Cecilia and her father's sponsorship; his freedom and future.

A read through of the first half of *Atonement*
shows how the writer's awareness of the different
potential paths before we arrive at Briony's crime
increases the drama, complexity and resonance of
the novel. Robbie hesitates on writing the letter
and attending the dinner – his future hanging
tantalizingly close. The mother has her own
complex reasons for not calling the police when
the twins disappear, or taking better care of her
household at a moment of crisis.

We can also see where the story is pushed past
what can at first seem a satisfactory ending. The
story carries the reader further than we could
have imagined; cousin Lola is barely on the radar
as the character in danger, and Briony could have
created a terrible scene on first reading the letter,
or on disturbing Cecilia and Robbie in the library.

 Back to Date

41
EMBRACE SOMETHING YOU DISLIKE

This might be in another character – such as the different attitudes expressed towards educating women in *Atonement*, for example, where Cecilia's mother Emily is amazed she has the gall to be disappointed at her poor exam results.

 Back to Date

44
VISIT A HALL OF MIRRORS

Atonement features an excellent mirror scene in chapter 9, when Cecilia changes three times for dinner.

 Back to Date

48
IMMERSE YOURSELF IN A DIFFERENT LANGUAGE

For example, one of the themes of *The Great Gatsby* could be said to be the corrupting power of excessive materialism, and thus it feels exactly right that a motorboat owned by Tom Buchanan is described as 'snub-nosed'.

 Back to Date

50
WATCH A BUSKER PERFORM

Harry Potter and the Philosopher's Stone is full of great supporting characters.

Harry's uncle Mr Dursley doesn't approve of imagination.

Dumbledore is the only wizard Voldemort is frightened of but is too noble to use his powers.

Despite being a wizard, Hagrid isn't supposed to do magic, and was expelled from Hogwarts. He's also twice as tall as everyone else.

 Back to Date

WORKS CITED

NOVELS

Ali, Monica, *Brick Lane* (London, 2004).

Doyle, Roddy, *Two Pints* (London, 2012).

Fitzgerald, F. Scott, *The Great Gatsby* (1926; London, 2000).

Freud, Esther, *Love Falls* (London, 2007).

Galloway, Janice, *The Trick is to Keep Breathing* (Edinburgh, 1989).

Hardy, Thomas, *The Mayor of Casterbridge* (1886; London, 2003).

Hunter, Erin, *Into the Wild, Warrior Cats Book 1* (New York, 2003).

Larsson, Steig, *The Girl with the Dragon Tattoo* (London, 2008).

McEwan, Ian, *Atonement* (London, 1999).

Rowling, J.K., *Harry Potter and the Philosopher's Stone* (1997; London, 2001).

Woolf, Virginia, *Orlando* (1928; London, 2004).

DRAMA

Sophocles, and Knox, Bernard, The Three Theban Plays: Antigone, Oedipus the King, Oedipus at Colonus (1982; New York, 1984).

NON-FICTION

Murakami, Haruki, *What I Talk About When I Talk About Running* (2008; London, 2009).

New Hart's Rules: The Handbook of Style for Writers and Editors (Oxford, 2005).

TV

Broen (The Bridge) Season 1 (SVT and DR, 2011).

Forbrydelsen (The Killing) Season 1 (DR1, 2007).

BEFORE YOU GO...

This book is inspired by editor and literary consultant Claire Wingfield's writing mentorships. You can find out more and sign up for Claire's e-newsletter at: www.clairewingfield.co.uk

If you would like professional feedback on your novel draft, information about online writing courses such as The Submissions Bootcamp or The Complete Book Marketing Toolkit, or to keep up to date with Claire's latest publications, please get in touch at: contact@clairewingfield.co.uk

You can also use the above address to send questions, comments or feedback on your writing dates.

If you feel this book has had a positive impact on your writing and would like to share the resource with other writers, please consider posting a review and sharing with your writing communities.

With thanks to Stephen Scarcliffe, Tracey Emerson, Kieran McLoughlin, designer Dan Prescott (www.couperstreet.com), Geoff Warwick and all the writers I have been fortunate enough to work with.

Happy Writing!

44124681R00077

Made in the USA
Middletown, DE
03 May 2019